Value Creating Strategies

For Information Technology (IT) Professionals

By Riazul Hasan, M.S.

First Edition, November 2007.

ISBN: 978-1-4357-0337-7

Value Creating Strategies
For Information Technology (IT) Professionals

Table of Contents

About the Author

Mr. Riazul Hasan has worked as an IT professional for several U.S based organizations as consultant and employee; Some of these organizations include Blue Cross of New York, Peterson, Howell & Heather Inc (PHH), Saudi Aramco, Honeywell Inc; J. & W. Seligman & Co. Inc; Computer task Group (CTG) and few other fortune 500 corporations such as MCI and Verizon Communications Inc. His work experience spans well over 35 years. Mr. Hasan has worked as a Project Manager, Systems Analyst, Software Developer, Network Administrator and Consultant in a variety of industries / applications which include hospital, mutual funds, auto leasing, hospital insurance, mortgage, billing, accounting, oil and telecommunications. Also – he worked as a consultant on a U.S Navy and U.S HUD projects. He survived three corporate mergers in the late nineteen nineties and the early part of year 2000. He holds a M.S in computer science from the Johns Hopkins University, Baltimore, Maryland, U.S.A. Mr. Hasan resides in the United States.

Outline

Section 1:   What is value?

An employee's worth is measured with respect to the amount of money that he generates or saves for his employers. Different scenarios are presented for identifying employees who are more valuable to their employers than others and whose services must be terminated in case there is a merger between two organizations. An employee who understands his employer's business is more likely to be retained when an employer must reduce his manpower resources for some valid reasons. This section covers a scenario for evaluating two well qualified IT professionals and out of which one must be terminated.

Section 2:   The secrets of "Value creating strategies" for IT professionals –
               unleashed

This section highlights various strategies which an employee could use effectively for upgrading his value or worth to his employers. Emphasis is placed on the comprehension of employer's business from marketing, financial, social, cultural and political perspectives. Employees who develop total awareness of their employer's business including regulatory compliance, legal obligations, corporate objectives and means to accomplish them offer more value to their employers than those who lack aforementioned characteristics. Employees should develop skills which are in short-supply. IT professionals should develop skills which others in a project team don't have it.

Section 3:   Development of business know-how! Is it essential?

Information Technology (IT) professionals need to develop a total awareness of their employer's business which is in fact a pre-requisite. They need to understand business user's environment and then apply technology to resolve their user related issue. Employers seeking IT professionals for employment always look for specific IT skills coupled with a strong business / industry background.

Section 4:   Value Creation Scenarios

This section identifies a scenario for creating value-added projects which should not only benefit an employer but also enhance an employee's value. Changes being incorporated into a process or network which has been functional and in place for some time pose a potential risk factor due to the presence of unknown factors. An example is cited of a Change Control Management Group (CCMG) which was established at a large corporation known by its fictitious name as XYZC, which has several offices in the east coast of the U.S. Any network or software change being implemented in Maryland might also impact processes in New York and Delaware. This section describes how the potential risks were identified and reported to the CCMG before changes were applied either to a Software or Network.

Section 5:   Other Value Creating Strategies (OVCS)

Some other Value Creation Scenarios include conversion of potential problems into value-added projects and Network Server Placement Strategies. Emphasis is placed on the acquisition of multiple skills and the ability to wear different hats when the situation arises. A Network Administrator or a Database Administrator who knows how to write script or develop code for reading a system's log and extracting useful information from it should enhance his / her value to their organizations. Again emphasis is placed on the identification of opportunities which would be beneficial to the organization and which could be transformed into value-added projects.

Section 6:   Case Study – IT value creating strategy in a hospital environment

This section places emphasis on learning a typical hospital environment and how a Database Administrator (DBA) could enhance his value by playing a useful role. Here is couple of practical useful hints and suggestions. A DBA needs to align his IT strategy with that of the hospital business strategy to associate value with his services. And this strategy should be focused on business processes which directly or indirectly either generate $$ for the hospital or attract new potential customers / patients and new growth oriented contractual opportunities which could have a significant impact on the overall revenue generating methodology. This section identifies hospital business processes which generate revenues and describes how a DBA should / could align his IT strategy with that of the business strategy for creating an effective value for his services. Role of a DBA is also discussed. A typical hospital organizational structure is also depicted which a DBA should not only understand their inter-relationship but also should be able to get a bigger picture of data flow between various hospital departments.

Section 7:   Some useful links

A summary of useful links, which every IT professional ought to know if he / she are serious in advancing their professional careers. For example – an IT Software developer working for a consulting company on a Medicare Insurance coverage project needs to know about how Medicare reimburses insurance companies when they file an insurance claim for a Medicare patient. The U.S Department of Health and Human Services and Centers for Medicare & Medicaid Services provides wealth of information in this respect.

Who should buy this book? – Target audience

Value Creating Strategies (V C S) for IT Professionals is a small useful synopsis written for Information Technology (IT) professionals (Systems Analysts, Network Administrators, Database Administrators, Programmers, Helpdesk Staff, Quality Assurance Analyst, IT Managers Etc). **V C S** contains some very practical scenarios aimed at generating value for your organization. VCS for IT professionals also includes a useful discussion as to how an IT professional could create value for himself working in a hospital environment.

If there are omissions or a specific idea being repeated or over emphasized, I would ask my gentle reader to forgive me and move on.

Lastly – if you should have some ideas for improving VCS for IT professionals, please drop me a line. I would respond to your email within three days. My email address is xplor371@yahoo.com .Thanks

Preface

People lose jobs when someone else could do their jobs. Employees, who are to be retained / terminated, are evaluated based upon their productivity / contribution to their organization. A Programmer with an in-depth know-how of banking regulations coupled with compliance regulatory requirements is very likely to be retained than just a programmer who lacks aforementioned know-how when a mass layoff is in the process of being planned. An IT Systems Analyst who understands company business and is fully technically competent to support corporate objectives in achieving their goals is more valuable than a Systems Analyst who is just technically competent without any knowledge of the related industry or applications. Employers seek IT professionals who posses a variety of skills and additionally are effective problem solvers / communicators. Let us consider an Information Technology job say a Business Analyst which right now appears to be in great demand based upon vacancies advertised on the internet. The job requirements of the above position are as follows:

- Documentation of business processes and creating business models
- Participation in the requirement gathering sessions and documentation of the same for review by process owners and future systems users
- Translation of above requirements into functional / system specifications and diagrams using Visio
- Establish business use cases and system use cases using standard CASE tools
- Manage and Control Changes pertaining to the business requirements documented in the early stages / phases
- Investigate / research scenarios for improving business processes aimed at lowering cost and upgrading productivity
- Establish use case scenarios for exceptions and document them for subsequent use

- Develop and implement Test Plans for all stages of systems and unit testing including integration testing
- Experience in measuring system's performance using standard tools
- Know-how of insurance industry an added advantage
- Ability to coordinate and act as a focal point of contact with different departments and stakeholders
- Experienced in giving presentations to Senior managers / executives
- Working knowledge of SDLC phases from project initiation to implementation

Excellent communication and inter-personal skills; knowledge of insurance industry is a distinct advantage; MBA from a recognized University highly preferable.

1. What is value?

A base ball player signs a multi million contract with New York Mets (NYM) after weeks of negotiation between the NYM owners and his agent. The agent argued that a multi million dollar deal was just right based on the revenues being generated by his client through TV commercials and at the ticket office. The value of the contract was $5.5 million. In other words – the player was valued at $5.5 million to the owners of NYM. What is value? How would you create a value for IT professionals?

Consider a scenario involving a merger in which an Investment company has to decide between two employees; one of them should be terminated; both of them are good, cooperative and have an exceptional positive attitude.

First Employee's background

A Software Engineer (Mr. SE) has been with the company for the past 5 years and is engaged in the following activities:

- Develops Applications in C++ and Java in a Linux operating environment
- Develops scripts using CSHELL for automating the collection of Systems Performance statistics
- Performs Systems / Application Tuning aimed at minimizing user response time and maximizing system's throughput
- Invokes Trace for resolving Application software problems
- Participates in Disaster Recovery, Workload Measurement and Risk Assessment exercises regularly

- Volunteers for resolving user related problems and maintains an excellent rapport with the user community
- Well Versed in the areas of business applications and specifically in the area of finance / investment and additionally pursuing a MBA program with concentration in Finance

SE has a B.S in Computer Science.

Second Employee's background

A Senior Software Engineer (Mr. SSE) has been with the company for the past 28 years and is primarily engaged in the following activities:

- Maintains the system's standard documentation manuals
- Interfaces with the users for resolving their problems
- Participates in meeting with the User Managers
- Negotiates with the vendors for arranging in-house technical training courses
- Arranges Company Picnics and has key contacts within the company
- Participates in Disaster Recovery Planning and implementation
- Manages Ad hoc Projects frequently

Mr. SSE has a B.A in History and has taken IT courses at a local community college. Also, if he can hang in there for another two years, he would be eligible for full company benefit package including a substantial pension.

Well – readers could easily guess as to who would keep his job and who would hit the road. The SE offers more value than the SSE. Generally – people lose jobs when some one else could do their jobs. Also, you can keep your job if you are knowledgeable about company business, culture, procedures / practices and additionally are able to apply technology effectively for resolving business problems. What are the secrets of value creating strategies?

2. The Secrets of "Value Creating Strategies" for IT Professionals - Unleashed

"Education is a companion which no future can depress, no crime can destroy, no enemy can alienate it and no nepotism can enslave. (Ropo Oguntimehin – The Internet)". Knowledge is acquired via education whether it is related to the application of Information Technology (IT) for resolving a business issue or some other pertinent situation. Essentially - IT **is employed to** process data which is the nucleus of a business organization upon which critical business decisions are made. **It is always beneficial for an IT professional to learn the business side of an employer without which no employee would be able to sustain an upper edge for corporate survivability in times of corporate financial crises**. Business knowledge of an entity is basically needed to create value added projects which should enhance an IT employee's value to his / her organization. In order to accomplish the aforementioned objective, an IT professional should create an awareness of legal, political, social, public and financial obligations of your employer and think of ways / means of creating value added projects which could either guide your employer in making cost effective decisions or equip your employer with facts and figures to be used for   making decisions aimed at protecting company image / reputation. Few other recommendations include:

- Know business data and its associated processes / procedures intimately (Refer to Development of business know-how! Is it essential below?) "

13

- Be familiar with the Acts of Congress and Standards affecting your Employer's business (Examples of regulations: SEC, FCC, FTC etc)

- Be aware of your company's future plan and direction

- Take courses on your own for gaining skills you lack

- Identify skills in your project teams which are essentially required but are lacking; try to acquire those skills on your own privately by hiring a hourly paid consultant to train you in those skills; you don't have to disclose your place of employment; example of courses include reading memory dumps, reading systems trace, debugging techniques etc in which most people struggle to get the concepts

- If possible, construct Data Flow Diagram (DFD) reflecting inter-process activity between local and remote processes. This should be of great help to you in understanding inter-process communication. This should help you not only in the area of risk management but also in managing systems / application changes

- Align your IT objectives with that of your employer's business objectives

- Always volunteer for projects that are visible and are important (Examples – Billing, Risk Management, Sales / Marketing, Procurement, Disaster Recovery, B2B, E-Commerce etc)

- Get connected with the user community / customers and establish an active working relationship with them; get to know their working environment including legal obligations such as federal / state government regulatory compliance and their business requirements; this should help you to plan your strategy from a technology perspective regarding its application for addressing hot issues

3. Development of business know-how! Is it essential?

Why should IT professionals develop an understanding of their employer's business and what are the potential benefits derived from this exercise?

A Civil Engineer (CE) is asked to design a large apartment complex to accommodate 200 tenants. The CE will gather facts / figures from his client including his specific requirements before addressing the planning / design phase of the project. In a similar fashion, an IT professional should have good feel of the client's environment and requirements before the application of technology for resolving user issues and problems.

A user environment involves automated / semi-automated / manual procedures, business / commercial / industrial / scientific processes, regulations, standards, external interfaces / connections and customers.

Generally, an IT professional should have a broad understanding of most of the entities described above coupled with a know-how of data, which has real value for the users. In fact employers seeking IT professionals prefer to hire some one with specific industry experience plus related IT expertise.

As an example – A software engineer developing a program in Java for processing inpatient admissions should do very well if his or her prior background includes work experience in a hospital environment.

A database administrator developing a patient database should do well with prior work experience in a hospital environment. Ability to wear multiple hats provides a built-in job security for IT professionals.

An IT Job Opening

B.S. in Computer Science, or equivalent experience; at least 2 years SAS Programming experience in a clinical environment; preference given to candidates with work experience either in a hospital environment or pharmaceutical industry.

Minimum Job Requirements

- Bachelor's degree or equivalent experience and/or education
- Three + years experience in programming
- Three + years experience in application development utilizing JAVA
- Three + years relational database experience
- Working knowledge of C/C++
- Solid experience in some of the following: J2EE (JAVA Servlets, JSP, EJB), UML and the Weblogic Application Server
- Strong written and oral communication skills
- Demonstrated track record of successful system and project implementations
- Preferred experience in a securities / Investment industry a big plus
- Successful completion of an analytical aptitude examination

Responsibilities and Duties

The Database Administrator (DBA) functions as a high-level technician working on a large complex multi RDMS environment (DB2 LUW, Z/OS DB2, Sybase, Oracle, MS SQL). As a member of a team of DBA's, the DBA should be capable of thinking independently, but operating in a team environment with a willingness to follow pre-defined IT policies to satisfy our customers. The candidate will be responsible for scripting, design/analysis, installation, monitoring, maintaining, troubleshooting, and tuning **DB2 UDB** databases for customers remotely and on-site. Project management responsibilities include identifying the scope of assigned projects, generating solutions to technical issues, reporting analysis and results, and providing deliverables in a timely and efficient manner. **The incumbent must be adaptive to the use of new software aids and programming techniques as they are acquired or adopted within IT. The DB2 Database Administrator may also** research and provide recommendations in support of procurement and development of database software and related tools.

Job Requirements

- Bachelor's degree or equivalent experience and/or education;
- Successful completion of an analytical aptitude exam;
- Must have solid experience in two of the following RDMS's: Oracle, MS SQL Server, Sybase, or DB2;
- Must have shell scripting experience on a UNIX platform (AIX or Linux);
- Data modeling and other Development DBA skills;
- Experience with complex RDMS implementations (e.g. large databases, Replication, Cluster-based) and other high availability environments;
- Must be self-motivated, a team player, and have a strong track record in customer satisfaction;
- Strong analysis/design capabilities along with demonstrated written/oral communication skills;
- Must have a propensity for problem-solving; and
- Demonstrated experience with successful system and project implementations.

- Three plus years of experience in a second RDMS (Sybase, Oracle, MS SQL, Z/OS DB2) preferred
- Prior work experience in an insurance industry as a DBA a big advantage

4. Value Creation Scenarios

One way to keep your job is to be able to wear more than one hat depending upon the environment in which you work. A systems engineer who is self-motivated, a team player, customer oriented and has had experience in the areas of software development, database design, technical writing, data modeling and is highly sensitive to the business needs is very likely to keep his job - should there be a massive lay off in the company.

How does this "value creating strategy" work and what are the things involved?

In order to explain the dynamics of this process, the author cites his real experience while working for a large corporation (assumed name XYZC), which was regulated by the Federal Communications Commissions (FCC). When the Telecommunication ACT of Congress was born and enforced in 1996, the barriers between phone companies were broken. Any local telephone company could provide long distance calling services and any long distance service provider could get into a local calling market.

XYZC was legally obliged by law to provide services to its competition for accessing its network and resources and failure to do would have had an adverse effect on its reputation plus a heavy fine.

XYZC Availability Issue

XYZC operated on a 24 x 7 basis and also availability of systems / network at all times was of paramount importance. There had been few cases when the XYZC's resources including systems and network were not available primarily due to the implementation of "change requests", which did not go through and the system / network had to be restored to its previous level / version resulting in loss of quality time.

Change Control Management Group (CCMG)

"Change requests" were administered and managed by the CCMG, which were also responsible for coordinating all changes with the process owners and external clients. Due to the complexity / diversity of hardware, network, processes and software distributed heterogeneously, CCMG did not have an automated procedure / process in place, which could facilitate CCMG in coordinating and implementing changes. An automated process was needed to manage change requests with minimal fatality.

CCMG Immediate Need-Identification of process owners

CCMG wanted to identify XYZC based processes which were engaged in sessions with local and **remote** processes and they wanted a report or reports reflecting every process and their session partners. The basic idea was to be able to contact Process Owners (PO) in advance so that PO's could participate in testing changes on a timely basis. CCMG were looking for any one to fulfill their needs on ASAP basis. Please see sample reports on Pages 22 and 23 respectively.

Minimize risk of failures caused by changes

In order to address the above immediate and crucial need, some one in the Network Support Services Group developed a script to read the system's log file and extract all the necessary information as per the CCMG requirements. It took the individual couple of late nights to develop the file while telecommuting.

The process was simple – for every process supplied by the user, the script would search the file and extract the session related data including cross domain session traffic.

Benefits Derived from the Project

The above mentioned script helped the CCMG not only in coordinating the changes effectively with all the process owners, but also in protecting XYZC against possible fines imposed by the FCC due to the unavailability of the network and its resources. This strategy also provided XYZC a protection against class action law suits originating from other Telecom carriers which should have had access to the XYZC network as per the contractual agreement.

Sample Report #1

Process or S/W To be modified	Interface Name (SW) (2)	Location (3)	IP Address / Port #	Operating System	Process Owner
Product Order (1)	Inventory Control	New York S.W	111.212.234.432 Port # 45	Linux	Smith Pager 212.234.3456
Distribute	Distribution	Washington N.W	111.234.789.432 Port # 46	Linux	Jordon Pager 202.234.3456
Sales	Sales	Philadelphia, PA	232.678.987.234 Port # 47	OS/390	John Hunter 734.456.3456 Call him
Accounts	Accounting	Baltimore, MD	890.678.892.234 Port # 56	Risc 6000	Call Judy 301.456.6789
(1) Product Order which was being modified interfaced with (2) four applications namely; Inventory Control, Distribution, Sales and Accounting in four cities as shown in (3). Process Owners were contacted to participate in testing when the change control was scheduled.					

XYZ Corporation   CCMG Report # 2

Change Control Management Group

Upgrade Router Interface Report for W/E July 25th, 2006

System: New York City - 800 Lexington Ave

Net ID(1)	Component to be upgraded (2)	Location (3)	IP Address	Operating Environment	Remarks	Network Coordinator
XYZ C WAN	CISCO Router	New York S.W	111.212.234.432	Linux	Test Connectivity & Interface	Smith Pager 212.234.3456
XYZ C WAN	CISCO Interface	Laurel N.W	111.234.789.432	Linux	Test Connectivity & Interface	Jordon Pager 202.234.3456
XYZ C WAN	CISCO Interface	Fairfax, VA	232.678.987.234	OS/390	Test Connectivity & interface	John Hunter 734.456.3456
XYZ C WAN	CISCO Interface	Balt, MD	890.678.892.234	Risc 6000	Test Connectivity & interface	Judy 301.456.6789

Notes: (1) Network Identification (2) Cisco Router to be upgraded at New York and interface / Connectivity to be tested at Washington DC,   New York City, Philadelphia and Baltimore, MD

Interpretation of Reports #1 and #2

Report # 1 shows an Application Programming Interface (API) "Product order" running on a server in New York which interacts with processes Distribution, Sales and Accounting running on servers in cities Washington DC, Philadelphia and Baltimore respectively.

Report #2 shows Network changes being applied to a CISCO Router located at New York City with interfaces or connections to Washington DC, Philadelphia PA and Baltimore, MD. The report also identifies Network Coordinator at each location which happens to be a key person at that location.

5. Other Value Creating Strategies (OVCS)

A) Converting Potential Problems into Projects

A large network has 20,000 physical components, which include modems, printers, cables, servers, repeaters etc; every physical component has an expected life provided by the manufacturer; if your employer does not have a database namely; (Product Expected Life Database), take the initiative of creating one; your value will go up rapidly.

This database namely; Product Expected Life Database (PELD) could be used for managing and predicting risk factors associated with servers and applications when they are either upgraded or undergo modifications under certain conditions.

Generate report(s) using the above Database as follows:

Anticipated Resource Failure Report(s) by Expiration Data & Location

Report # 1

Product	Expiration Date	Hours-Days left	Remarks
Printer	07/01/ 2006	59 Days	To be replaced
Server	09/01/ 2006	150 plus days	No action required
Router	01/01/2008	over 400 days	No action required

Report # 2

Product	Expiration Date	Hours-Days left	Location	IP Address
Printer	07/01/ 2006	59 Days	750 5th Ave NYC	111.234.234.001
Server	09/01/ 2006	150 plus days	1230 2nd Street, NYC	111.234.234.011
Router	01/01/2008	over 400 days	102 8th Street	143.234.567.999

Report # 3

Product	Expiration Date	Hours-Days left	Applications	IP Address
Server	07/01/ 2006	59 Days	Order Processing System	111.234.234.001
Server	09/01/ 2006	150 plus days	Purchasing	111.234.234.011
Server	01/01/2008	over 400 days	Inventory Control	143.234.567.999

Benefits derived from the project

a) You would be able to predict accurately when certain network components would fail or likely to fail based on the current date and the actual expiration date.

b) You would also be able to predict accurately the impact of equipment failure on business processes and location, if a correlation could be established between equipment, location deployed and software supported.

c) By generating an "Equipment Failure Report" on a monthly basis, you are alerting senior managers and executives as to which process or equipment might be disabled in a specific time frame and its impact on the user community and business; now it becomes management's responsibility to prevent that event from occurring

B) Network Server Placement Strategy

Since a Network Server provides a service to its clients, its physical placement plays a crucial role not only in its availability / accessibility but also in its performance which are essential factors in minimizing network delays. Try to place Network Server on the Backbone which should allow two or more subnets to exchange data with minimum delay.

Try to identify appropriate server placement algorithm to justify your Server Placement strategy. This should add value to your profile. Send a questionnaire to the key users and IT Managers and analyze their responses statistically. Give a presentation on your findings to Management. Some of the questions for your survey are reflected in a table as shown below.

#	Criteria	Remarks
1.	# of Users – 500 to 650	Some out of state users
2.	Type of Traffic	FTP, Interactive Graphics
3.	Response Time	Under 3 seconds or less
4.	Number of Interfaces	Four Interfaces, New York, Baltimore, Washington DC, Los Angles, CA
5.	Data Sharing between departments	Need to assess the risk factors associated with this; if a server is down, it will affect both the departments
6.	Bandwidth requirements	Needs high bandwidth to accommodate FTP & Graphics
7.	Mainframe Connectivity	Yes – with New York
8.	Back up Servers	A requirement
9.	Availability	24 x 7
10.	Security / Fire wall	Required

Benefits derived from the project

Above table is a suggestion; actual service requirements depend upon your IT shop environment. A service placement requires an in-depth study and this study should take into consideration all possible risk factors, which could create potential problems. A well-thought strategy should make you look good and add value to your profile.

C) Summarize Problems by Category – Problem Management

Examine your Systems Logs (Last three months or more) and extract all the severe / fatal errors and summarize them for sharing with the helpdesk and call center; if possible, draw a graph using Excel.

Report # 1

Error Code	Error Description	Freq	From	To
001	Server Configuration Error	150	04/01/2006	06/30/2006
002	Network Card Error, Invalid Configuration	200	04/01/2006	06/30/2006
003	Server memory fault	250	04/01/2006	06/30/2006

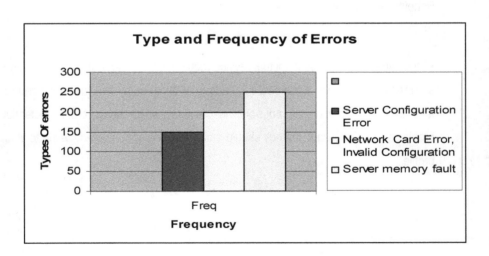

Report # 2

Application / system	Description	Fatal Errors Or Outages	Period
Inventory	Inventory of Manufactured Products	350	01/06 – 05/06
Billing	Customer Billing / Invoices	200	01/05 – 12/05
Sales Support	Sales & Services	250	01/05 – 12/05
Purchasing	Procurement Factory Items	400	01/06 – 05/06

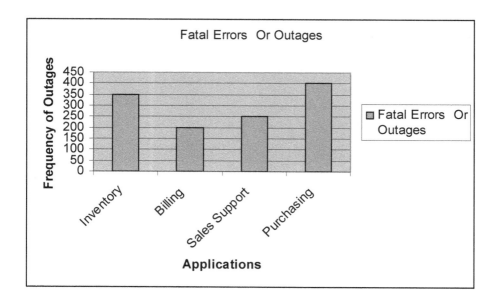

D) Disaster Recovery (D/R)

Get involved with the Disaster Recovery Project; it's a learning process and a value-added project.

This project should support the scenario that "If the data center is struck with a major disaster, the systems / network should be recovered at a remote location and be available for processing within 24 hours". A D/R offers an excellent opportunity to learn the operating environment of the organization including critical processes, resources and applications.

E) Information Technology (IT) Audit

Get involved with IT audit and develop expertise in this respect; if you are familiar with business processes, its culture and have contacts with process owners, you would be an excellent choice for inclusion on this project.

F) Resource Utilization

Undertake a resource utilization study involving servers, printers, work stations, routers etc and summarize them with their types and building locations; $$ could be saved in canceling license renewals, maintenance contracts and other overheads, if the equipment is not being used – (Source of these reports depends upon your specific environment).

Resource Utilization Report					
XYZC – Analysis of Servers by Applications, IP address, Facility and Location					
Server Type	Application supported	Status	IP Address	Office address or Facility	Location
IBM	Inventory	Active	111.222.333.444	Finance Department	Washington, DC
IBM	Sales	Active	111.212.333.445	Marketing Department	Boston, MA
GE	GL	Active	111.212.334.435	Accounts Dept	New York
IBM	Billing	Active	111.212.336.436	Billing	Troy, MI
IBM	Banking	Active	111.212.332.431	Banking	Baltimore
MS	Manufacturing	Active	111.212.331.431	N.J Plant	NJ
MS	Manufacturing	Inactive	111.212.331.430	N.J Plant	NJ
IBM	Sales	Active	111.212.333.441	Marketing Department	Boston, MA
IBM	Sales	Active	111.212.333.489	Marketing Department	Boston, MA
MS	Manufacturing	Inactive	111.212.331.234	N.J Plant	NJ

Statistical Summary

# of IBM Servers = 6 Status Active = 8 # of Applications (Sales) = 3
# of MS Servers = 3 Status Inactive = 2 # of Applications (GL) = 1
# of GE Servers = 1 # of Applications (Inventory) = 1
# of Applications (Billing) = 1
# of Applications (Manufacturing) = 3
# of Applications (Banking) = 1

Please note that location and facility statistics could also be summarized by cities and facility respectively.

The above report could be used for accounting, assets management, auditing, IT planning and Inventory management functions.

G) Risk Management & its Impact on other Processes

Undertake a comprehensive study regarding risk management and its impact on resources, processes and manpower. The objectives of the study should be:

(1) To ensure that the systems are available and accessible on a 7 x 24 basis

(2) To pre-plan alternatives for the Just-in-case situations when the resources are not available for supporting mission critical business applications.

If a server is disabled, its associated processes (Applications) would not be accessible. Report #1 on page 33 shows the impact analysis as to which applications would not be accessible and how many end users will be affected due to the outage. Data for the report could be extracted from the Network Logs, summarized and reported.

XYZ Corporation   CMC Report # 1

Change Control Management Group

Risk Management Report by Server / Applications

System: New York City – 800 Lexington Ave

Server Type	Application	# of End User Seats (2)	IP Address	Session Partner / Interface (1)	Location
IBM	Inventory	50	111.222.333.444	Sales, GL, Billing, Banking	Washington DC
IBM	Sales	150	111.212.333.445	Sales, GL, Billing, Inventory	Boston, MA
GE	GL	30	111.212.334.435	Sales, Banking, Billing, Inventory	New York
IBM	Billing	200	111.212.336.436	Sales, Banking, Inventory, GL	Troy, MI
IBM	Banking	75	111.212.332.431	Sales, Inventory, GL, Billing	Baltimore

Application Inventory executes from server 111.222.333.444 located in Washington DC and interacts with applications Sales, General Ledger (GL), Billing and Banking placed on servers in Boston, New York, Troy MI, and Baltimore MD respectively. A total of 505 end user seats will be affected.

Interpretation of the Risk Management Reports

Report #1

If the server 111.222.333.444   in Washington, which has the executable code for application "Inventory " is disabled, then this scenario would impact other applications running on servers located in cities Boston MA, New York, Troy MI and Baltimore respectively. A total of 505 users will be affected by the incident.

H) IP Addresses Utilization Report

If you realize that there is a great demand of IP addresses and that you are experiencing difficulties in getting hold of IP addresses due to shortage, you could address this problem by writing a quick utility by capturing data pertaining to IP addresses active in use and assigned by underutilized as described in the report on the next page:

IP Addresses Utilization Report
Contact # 212-555-8090
XYZ Corporation

IP Address	Hardware Type	Last Access Date	Location	Remarks
111.234.234.001		July 4th, 2006	999 5th Ave NYC	
111.234.234.011		July 4th, 2006	999 2nd Street, NYC	
143.234.567.001	IBM Server	July 4th, 2001	999 8th Street,	Never accessed for the past five years
143.234.567.002		July 4th, 2006	999 5th Ave NY	
143.234.567.003		July 4th, 2006	999 5th Ave NY	
143.234.567.004	IBM Server	July 4th, 2000	999 5th Ave NY	Disable – reuse IP address
143.234.567.005		July 4th, 2006	999 5th Ave NY	
143.234.567.006		July 4th, 2006	999 5th Ave NY	
143.234.567.007		July 4th, 2006	999 5th Ave NY	
143.234.567.008		July 4th, 2006	999 5th Ave NY	
143.234.567.009	MS Server	July 4th, 2002	999 5th Ave NY	Never accessed since the last 4 years
143.234.567.010		July 4th,	999 5th Ave NY	

		2006		
143.234.567.011		July 4th, 2006	999 5th Ave NY	
143.234.567.012		July 4th, 2006	999 5th Ave NY	
143.234.567.013		July 4th, 2006	999 5th Ave NY	

6. Case Study – IT value creating strategy in a hospital environment

Let us undertake a case study involving a typical hospital known as the XYZ Hospital. Let us also assume that you have been working in IT department of the hospital as a Data Base Administrator (DBA) in an Oracle environment. What should you do different to make you valuable and visible?

Here is couple of practical useful hints and suggestions. You need to align your IT strategy with that of the hospital business strategy to associate value with your services. And this strategy should be focused on business processes which directly or indirectly either generate $$ for the hospital or attract new potential customers / patients and new growth oriented contractual opportunities which could have a significant impact on the overall revenue generating methodology.

Before the above issue namely - the alignment of IT strategy with that of hospital business strategy is discussed, let me quickly summarize very briefly the basic responsibilities of a DBA:

- Installation and configuration of Oracle9i Database
- Management of User accounts and their privileges
- Storage / Performance Management

- Management of Tables and Indexes
- Establishment of Backup and Recovery Procedures
- Oracle - Performance Management & Tuning
- SQL – Programming Support
- Plus other user related activities

All the steps mentioned above are technically oriented and have no value for the user community. For example a user does not care as to how an Oracle database table is organized or stored. Either the users don't see any monetary value in the above mentioned tasks or they can't relate or link the above tasks to their own on-going business related activities.

Let us now address the IT / business alignment strategy. It involves three steps as follows:

a) Analysis of critical business processes
b) Strategy – Construction
c) Strategy implementation and measuring its effectiveness

Analysis of critical business processes

It is important to know the business environment, its resources & services and the interaction between and within different departments of an organization. Without this know-how, an IT professional would not be able to align IT strategy with that of the business strategy for optimum results. Your goal should be focused on learning about the XYZ Hospital Center and its operating environment, business partners, culture, procedures (example – inpatient admission), processes (example – patient billing), government regulations (example – Medicare claim regulation), vendors, and other pertinent information.

Learning implies getting a broader and a better picture of various activities associated with the hospital, health care government agencies and their regulations / procedures. The basic idea is to be able to identify various departments of XYZ Hospital Center and their inter-departmental activities including data flow between them internally and with other vendors externally. All the facts / figures gathered in the analytical phase should be documented for subsequent use.

A quick review of the XYZ Hospital Center shown on the last page of the book depicts its organizational structure which comprises sixteen departments each department performing a certain specific functional activity. Each department exchanges data / information with other departments and consequently is inter-dependant upon other departments for their processing needs. In other words – data flows between various departments and is processed / re-processed depending upon certain criteria for meeting the business objectives of the XYZ Hospital Center. A data flow oriented XYZ Hospital Center billing process is being displayed on the last page of this book. This document assumes that a patient is covered by two insurance policies (Medicare plus a private insurer). The XYZ hospital center files a claim for services provided by the hospital to Centers for Medicare & Medicaid Services administered by the U.S Department of Health and Human Services for Medicare and a private Insurance company. After being reimbursed by the two insurers, the patient is billed for the difference which should be the patient's liability.

Hospital Regulations

A hospital is administered in accordance with certain well defined rules and regulations. Hospital regulatory agencies include United States Department of Health and Human Services, Centers for Medicare & Medicaid Services and Maryland Health Care

Commission (For the State of Maryland). Please note that all states within the U.S have their own separate departments.

Critical business processes or functional activities should include the following:

Patient's safety and security as established by law

- Patients care and provision of medical related services
- Patients / Insurance billing
- Insurance claims processing
- Pharmaceutical Services
- Government initiated programs (Medicare, Medicaid, Home health care, Senior care and other pertinent services)
- Doctors / Nursing Services
- Accounts Receivable / Payable

IT professionals including DBA(s) should be able to envisage a bigger picture of the entities, institutions, and the government agencies which should interface / interact with the XYZ Hospital Center for exchanging pertinent information related to patient. As an example – The National Institute of Health (NIH) would be highly interested in receiving data pertaining to a patient's disease involving cholera and who recovered after receiving medical treatment at the XYZ Medical Center.

Strategy – Construction

How do we align IT strategy with business strategy?

CIO's should not be establishing policies and guidelines for IT / business alignment.

Professional staff at a lower level should be engaged in aligning IT strategy with that of business due to their intimate know-how of business processes and their inter-dependence on the IT. The four stages of the alignment cycle are:

Planning, establishing a new process model or re-engineering an existing business model with adequate resources and service levels, managing the business model to ensure the service levels are met and lastly measuring or quantifying the business model / re-engineered processes for results.

Let us analyze some practical business functional / activities which must be executed all the time either for business reasons. The following revenue generating business processes appear to be good candidates for IT strategic alignment and involvement:

Identification of business processes for IT alignment

#	Process Name	Process Description	Business Value	Rational For selection
1.	Patient Admission (PA)	Hospital in-patient admissions	High	Generates $$ for the hospital
2.	Patient Transfer	Used for transferring patients from one room to another	High	Generates $$ for the hospital
3.	Patient Insurance Claim	Used for processing claims against Insurance companies	High	Generates $$ for the hospital
4.	Medicare eligibility	As per law, Medicare eligibility must be verified before filing a claim	High	Legal as per the U.S Government
5.	Patients Billing	Process Patient's bills for services provided	High	Generates $$ for the hospital

Let us consider # 3 and 5 described above as candidates for IT strategic alignment. Both Patient Insurance Claim and Patients Billing are revenue generating processes. Readers could argue that these two processes are already automated using state of art technology and what else could be done for an IT strategic alignment? OK. That's a fair argument or a concern. Consider the following scenario.

An IT performance Analyst who has recently joined the XYZ Medical Center asked the IT operations Manager during a new employee's orientation session the following questions:

1. How many insurance claims (transactions) are handled by the system every month?
2. How long does it take to process a single claim?
3. What is the breakdown by the type of claim (Inpatient / Outpatient)?

Pre optimization Insurance Claims and Patients billing statistical facts / figures report

	Process	Transaction Rate	# of Transactions	Target Goal
1	Patient Insurance Claim	One Transaction every twenty minutes	30KTransactions per month	Goal is to complete 40K transaction monthly
2	Patients Billing	One transaction every ten minutes	35K Transactions per month	Goal is to complete 50K transaction monthly

To address question 3 above, outpatients comprise 55% of the patient's traffic while inpatients comprise 45% of the traffic. The targeted goals of 40k and 50k transactions monthly corresponding to the Patient Insurance claim and patients billing respectively involves a higher throughput rate to accommodate a substantial increase in the number of transactions. This is a challenging assignment and requires some careful planning from the IT Group. Also- the user community should be asked for their active involvement in all phases of optimization.

Strategy Implementation and measuring its effectiveness

Let us assume that the DBA has been assigned as a Project Manager (PM) to lead the Project. The primary objective of the project is to optimize the system in its entirety to meet the target goals namely; 40k and 50k transactions respectively. Continue here

The PM should assemble a team of experienced IT professionals involving a Network Administrator, DBA, S/W developer, Systems Analyst, Quality Assurance Analyst, Performance Management expert and two or more representatives from the user departments and then embark upon a plan aimed at meeting the stated objectives. Results should be quantified and a record maintained to demonstrate progress systematically.

Since the systems architecture is composed of several hardware and software components, each subject matter expert of the above team should re-examine his own specific area of interest and come with a practical doable plan for addressing the above stated objectives vis-à-vis; ability to process 40,000 and 50,000 transactions for supporting Patient Insurance Claim and Patients Billing respectively. And this should be the primary focus of the team.

Let us examine briefly the path of a transaction from its inception to completion. Let us examine a typical patient's billing transaction. A billing analyst invokes a transaction of a patient who was discharged from the XYZ hospital. And also let us assume that Patient (Mr. Patrick or Mr. P) was an inpatient and he stayed in the hospital for 4 days. Before Mr. P is billed for the amount due, the following sequence of events (Manual & automated) should occur:

- Hospital will all identify all charges for products and services provided to Mr. P during his stay 4 day in the hospital including room charges, drugs provided, provision of nursing care, laboratory services, doctors / nurses fees etc
- Hospital will file a claim (electronic claim) with Medicare for Mr. P and the other private Insurer
- Medicare and the private insurer will reimburse the XYZ medical center a certain amount depending upon Mr. P's eligibility
- The hospital will send Mr. P an invoice for the balance (Example – assume total charges for hospital stay were $10,000; reimbursement from Medicare and private insurers were $7,000.00; Mr. P must be billed for $3,000.00

The Project Manager and his team should identify bottlenecks in the above events and address those areas for improvement. The bottlenecks (Technical & Process oriented) could be due to several reasons described below:

1. Inefficient Database Table organization involving too much I/O bound activities
2. Delay caused by Medicare processing and / or the private Insurer
3. Insufficient memory to process claims based on the systems log file
4. Too many "waits" involving resources remote and local based upon the transaction log
5. Network congestion caused by Network errors based upon the network logs
6. Server(s) not available on a timely basis
7. Slow FTP caused by inconsistent network performance
8. Too many connectivity related issues based upon transaction / network logs

9.   Billing software problems

10.   Plus other technical problems depending upon the H/W and S/W environment

A team effort coupled with the management commitment is required to address the above problems in a timely orderly fashion.

Regarding the role of a DBA

A Database Administrator's position is very critical for the business and its survival. A DBA controls one of the most important resources, which holds the corporate data / information. A DBA who understands corporate business very well including interpretation of the pertinent Acts of Congress, laws & regulations and business trends could play a lead role for protecting and promoting corporate business. A DBA should look beyond his position and needs to understand business culture, specific business trends, potential business needs and direction and accordingly customize his functional activities to support the corporate business. Briefly stated – a DBA should anticipate new requirements by providing a variety of reports, which he thinks could be useful from the business perspective.

As per Table 1 on page 46, a hospital is regulated by the U.S Department of Health and Human Services and a state government agency such as Maryland Health Care Commission, State of Maryland.

Typically – a hospital DBMS operating in an Oracle9i environment should be able to address following SQL triggered queries:

1. Generate a report for all patients entered as inpatients covered by Medicare and another insurance company during the year 2001 – 2004 living in the zip code 21228 and were diagnosed as insomnia patients;

2. Generate a report for all patients covered by Medicare during the year 2001 – 2005 who underwent open heart surgery and survived;

3. Generate a report for all patients covered by the HHC and were being treated as outpatients during the year 1999-2001;

4. Generate a report to reflect the effect of generic medicine XXXXXX on all outpatients treated during the period March 2004 to present; this report is required by a class action law suit by the patients and the XYZ Hospital is party to this suit;

5. Generate a report showing all Federal employees covered by New York Life Insurance Company and who received X –Ray services from this hospital during the year 1998;

6. Generate a report reflecting all outpatients treated by Dr. John Grook, M.D during the year 2004 before he was fired;

7. Generate a report showing all patients who received Emergency Care Services and who resided in zip codes 21228, 21339, 21145, 21999 and 21345;

8. Generate a report showing all patients who received Emergency Care Services and who resided in zip codes 21228, 21339, 21145, 21999 and 21345 and used hospital Ambulance services in the year 2005;

9. Generate a report for all patients entered as inpatients covered by Medicare and another Insurance company during the year 2001 – 2004 living in the zip code 21229 and 21778 and were diagnosed as mentally retarded;

10. Extract from the Database all inpatients who stayed in the XYZ hospital center for over 21 days, covered by Blue Cross (primary), were U.S DOD employees and lived in the Zip Codes 21227, 21339, 21145, 21999 and 21345 and were diagnosed as suffering from brain tumor and had multiple insurance plan coverage ;

11. Extract and report all patients between the years 1999 – 2003 residing in the Washington DC area covered by Mutual of New York (MONY) and Medicare and diagnosed as brain dead and whose primary physician was Dr. Grook M.D; this report is required by July 2nd 2006 for initial review; final version will be required by July 10th, 2006 as per the court order (Dr. John Grook M.D versus surviving patients – class action law suit) ;

12. Extract all inpatients who stayed in the hospital XYZ hospital center between the years 2000 – 2004 and whose claims were denied by the insurance companies and who also happened to have been treated by two other hospitals in the New York City area during the same period.

Finally – the author has described some of the strategies which he successfully implemented during his IT career and was able to survive corporate politics and mergers. However, the creation of opportunities depends upon your individual circumstances including corporate culture, future corporate plans, and relationship with the user community and your immediate supervisor. Technical knowledge and business knowledge of the industry will earn you respect.

Table 1: Cross Reference Summary by Application / Industry –To be used as one of the sources for learning your employer's business (See Note 1 below)

#	Application or Industry	Source or Agency	Comments
1.	Medicare / Medicaid Claims	U.S Department of Health and Human Services and Centers for Medicare & Medicaid Services	Also information available from U.S Social Security Administration Check the Act of Congress related to Medicare / Medicaid
2.	Automobile/ Life/ Health Insurance	State Insurance Department	Example – State of Maryland Insurance Commissioner

3.	Wall Street financial information	Securities and Exchange Commission (SEC)	Very bulky book – may be reviewed at the public library
4.	Telecommunication / Telephone / Cable	(FCC),Check also ACT of Congress related to Telecom Act of Congress (ACT)	Most Telecom S/W is developed by U.S based Telecordia
5.	Traffic / Transportation / Highway, U.S Ports	Federal Highway Administration and U.S Dept. of Transportation	Check also FHA ACT
6.	Hospital System	United States Department of Health and Human Services	Also contact. For Maryland, Maryland Health Care Commission; Centers for Medicare & Medicaid Services
7.	Food / Drug Systems	U.S Food & Drug Administration	ACT related to Food & Drug
8.	Home health care / Senior Care	Maryland Home Health Care Agency(HHCA)	Every State has a HHCA, Check also ACT of congress
9.	Banking	U.S Federal Reserve Board, Federal Deposit Insurance Corporation (FDIC)	ACT of Congress related to Banking & Finance
10.	Customs / Excise	U.S Dept. of Customs	ACT of Congress
11.	Taxes	U.S Internal Revenue Services	ACT of Congress
12.	Energy	U.S Department of Energy	ACT of Congress
13.	Imports, Exports, Economics, International Trade, demographic data,	U.S Department of Commerce U.S Dept of Customs	ACT of Congress

		Standards & Measure		
14	Single / Multiple family housing mortgage, FHA Loans	U.S Housing and Urban Development Agency	Also check Fannie Mae -- ACT of Congress
15.	Immigration & Naturalization	U.S Department of Immigration	ACT of Congress
16.	Food Manufacturing Standards	U.S Department of Food & Drug Administration	ACT of Congress
17.	Auto Industry Manufacturing	National Institute of Standards & Technology	WWW.cfla.org/ll/standard.htm
18.	Medical and Behavioral Research	National Institute of Health (NIH)	NIH reports to U.S Department of Health and Human Services
19.	Environment, Clean Air, Pollution, Waste Management, Water quality	U.S Dept. of Environment Protection Agency (EPA)	ACT of Congress, Clean Water Act, Nuclear Waste Policy Act
20.	Protection of water resources, environment, infrastructure, homeland security and War support	Army Corps of Engineers	http://www.usace.army.mil

7. Some other Useful Links are described below:

A. http://www.usa.gov/Agencies/Federal/Executive.shtml

B. http://www.usa.gov/Agencies/State_and_Territories.shtml
(Insurance / Hospitals / Highways)

C. http://www.usa.gov/Agencies/Federal/All_Agencies/index.shtml

D. http://www.dhmh.state.md.us/   (State of Maryland Dept. of Health & Mental Hygiene)

E. http://www.mdinsurance.state.md.us/documents/AutoTaskForce02-10-05.pdf
(Auto Insurance)

F. http://www.mdot.state.md.us/   (State of Maryland, Dept. of Transportation)

XYZ Hospital Center - Organizational Structure

Hospital President

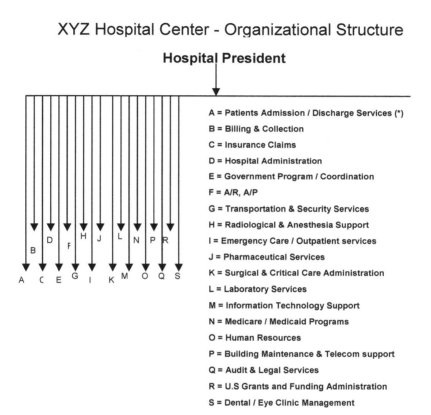

A = Patients Admission / Discharge Services (*)

B = Billing & Collection

C = Insurance Claims

D = Hospital Administration

E = Government Program / Coordination

F = A/R, A/P

G = Transportation & Security Services

H = Radiological & Anesthesia Support

I = Emergency Care / Outpatient services

J = Pharmaceutical Services

K = Surgical & Critical Care Administration

L = Laboratory Services

M = Information Technology Support

N = Medicare / Medicaid Programs

O = Human Resources

P = Building Maintenance & Telecom support

Q = Audit & Legal Services

R = U.S Grants and Funding Administration

S = Dental / Eye Clinic Management

(*) Each Alphabet either represents a department or a unit within the hospital headed by a Vice President or a Director

An Information Technology Department must understand each department's processing needs in its entirety which is an essential factor for success.

XYZ Hospital
Center
Patients Billing
Process

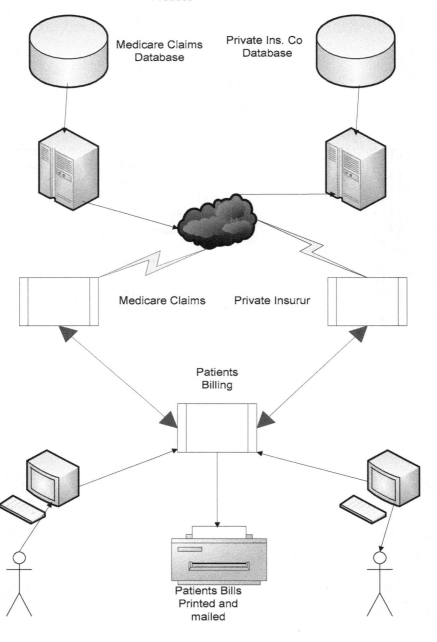

Medicare Claims
Database

Private Ins. Co
Database

Medicare Claims

Private Insurur

Patients
Billing

Patients Bills
Printed and
mailed

www.ingramcontent.com/pod-product-compliance
Lightning Source LLC
Chambersburg PA
CBHW051216050326
40689CB00008B/1336